W9-CNJ-906

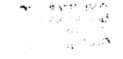

Be Smart About Shopping

The Critical Consumer and Civic Financial Responsibility

Kathiann M. Kowalski

$
BE SMART
ABOUT
MONEY
AND
FINANCIAL
LITERACY

Enslow Publishers, Inc
40 Industrial Road
Box 398
Berkeley Heights, NJ 07922
USA
http://www.enslow.com

This book is dedicated to my daughter, Laura Meissner.

Copyright © 2014 by Kathiann M. Kowalski

Library of Congress Cataloging-in-Publication Data

Kowalski, Kathiann M., 1955–
    Be smart about shopping : the critical consumer and civic financial responsibility / Kathiann M. Kowalski.
        pages cm. — (Be smart about money and financial literacy)
        Summary: "Discusses smart shopping and the critical consumer, including basic money choices, prioritizing financial decisions, comparison shopping, making smart purchasing choices, protecting against identity theft, and civic financial responsibility"— Provided by publisher.
        Includes bibliographical references and index.
        ISBN 978-0-7660-4283-4
        1. Home economics—Accounting. 2. Consumer education. I. Title.
        TX326.K68 2014
        640.73—dc23
                                    2013000698

Future editions:
Paperback ISBN: 978-1-4644-0509-9
EPUB ISBN: 978-1-4645-1263-6
Single-User PDF ISBN: 978-1-4646-1263-3
Multi-User PDF ISBN: 978-0-7660-5895-8

Printed in the United States of America

112013 Bang Printing, Brainerd, Minn.

10 9 8 7 6 5 4 3 2 1

Contents

Throughout the book, look for this logo 🙂 for smart financial tips and this logo 🙁 for bad choices to avoid. Also, don't forget to "Do the Math" at the end of each chapter.

It's Your Money

"Get ready, get set, get shopping!" urged the *Teen Vogue* ads. No, the magazine wasn't promoting a new reality TV show. It was hyping Back-to-School Saturday, an August shopping event aimed at teens. "We're trying to create a moment of imagination and motivation," *Teen Vogue*'s Jason Wagenheim told the *New York Times*.

The magazine was also aiming to rack up revenues for its advertising partners. The promotion included Aéropostale, American Eagle Outfitters, Express, Staples, and other stores. For these and many other companies, teens are big business. The 2012 Harris Poll YouthPulse study found that American youths aged eight to twenty-four have $211 billion in purchasing power.

While the entire youth market is huge, individual teens have limited funds. To get the most for your money, become a critical consumer.

Buy the Book—and More!

Even if *Teen Vogue* didn't tout Back-to-School Saturday, you'd almost certainly spend money over your summer vacation and throughout the school year, too. You probably need new school books and supplies. Maybe you'd shop for new clothes or shoes. And don't forget fun reading, music, games, and going out with friends. Life isn't all about school!

Of course, buying things takes money. Money is anything that a society accepts as payment for goods or services. The form of money, or currency, depends on your location. In the United States, for example, the dollar ($) is the basic unit of currency. Most of Europe uses the Euro (€). China currently uses the yuan (¥), and Japan uses the yen (¥).

Money would be worthless if it couldn't buy things now or in the future for you or others. Perhaps you work at a part-time job. Maybe you also get money as an allowance or from gifts. No matter how you get money, you can do three basic things with it:

- You can spend money.
- You can save money.
- You can give money away.

Smart financial planning usually involves using some money in each of these ways.

What's Behind the Price Tag?

The United States operates primarily on a market economy. This means, generally speaking, that producers offer goods and services for a price. Goods are physical products or, as the magazine *The Economist* likes to say, "things you can drop on your toe." Services are things providers do for people. Examples include teaching, babysitting, or health care.

Sometimes buyers and sellers negotiate on price. Examples may include large transactions, such as buying a car or a home. Negotiations can also occur in smaller transactions, such as arranging to cut someone's grass or shopping at a farmer's market.

For most day-to-day transactions, however, businesses determine the price. Companies need to pay expenses, including materials, salaries, rent, utilities, and other costs. Companies also aim to earn a profit for their owners or investors.

In general, the higher the demand is for a good or service, the more a seller can charge. Demand is usually higher for desirable items that are scarce. For example, high-tech gadgets usually debut at a high price because demand is often highest then. According to *ABC News,* Apple's iPhone 5 cost $199 when the company introduced it in September 2012. Four months later, Wal-Mart had it on sale for $127—one-third off the retail price. Conversely, when the supply is plentiful, sellers may lower prices. When increased drilling and warmer weather swelled natural gas inventories in 2012, for example, prices came down.

As an individual, you have little power over how companies set prices. Usually, however, you can decide whether you're willing to pay those prices. If not, you have several options. You can buy from someone else. You can borrow or do something yourself. You can postpone the purchase. Or, you might do without it altogether. What you choose depends on your priorities.

Just as you need regular physical check-ups, take time now and then to review your financial situation. Consider where you want to be financially now, five years from now, and ten years after that. Think about that big picture whenever you make significant purchasing decisions. If you buy a car right now, for example, how will that affect your financial situation in the future?

Remember the fable about the ant and the grasshopper? While the ant worked hard, the grasshopper partied and played. Because he hadn't planned for the future, the grasshopper starved when winter came.

Don't let future financial needs catch you by surprise. Learn financial skills now that will serve you for a lifetime.

Be Smart About Shopping

Now it's your turn to "Do the Math." The end of each chapter features a math or word problem. Use what you learned in the chapter to help you answer the questions. The right math will help you make the right financial decisions.

Do the Math

- As best as you can remember, make a list of all your back-to-school purchases for this school year. Note the approximate price you paid for each item. Then calculate the total.

- Which items were specifically required by your school, such as certain notebooks or texts? Which other items do you use solely for school, such as a backpack or a gym bag?

- Which of your purchases do you use for school and other purposes, too? Clothing might be one example.

- How do you feel about each of your back-to-school purchases now? Which were good choices? Are there any that you regret? How much money could you have saved without them?

Decide on Priorities

Consumers face a basic economic dilemma: We don't have enough money for everything. Smart consumers make sure they can pay for the most important items before spending for other things.

Needs vs. Wants

Categories of spending are not all equal. Some spending fulfills basic needs. Needs are things you must have to survive and function normally in society. Wants are things you desire above and beyond basic needs.

Everyone needs food, clothing, and a place to live. As a teen, you also need books and supplies for school. You need transportation to and from school, clubs, and any part-time job. You need opportunities for social activities, too.

Within each category, there's a range between what you absolutely need and what you might want. You need clean clothing that fits comfortably. A new leather jacket or another pair of designer jeans would be a luxury—something you want but don't need.

Similarly, we all need to socialize with friends. Hiking, playing ball, or getting together to watch videos are low-cost ways to satisfy this need. Attending a professional sporting event or skiing at a resort would cost much more. Most of their expense would fall into the category of something you want but don't necessarily need.

Wanting things beyond basic needs is okay. Just make sure that you can meet all your basic needs. After that, decide how much you want certain things compared to others.

Why Do You Want It?

Simply stated, consumers want things that they believe will make life better. Many factors influence those beliefs.

Friends play an obvious role when you choose group activities. Your peers probably also shape your preferences in clothing, gadgets, and other items. You see what they have and listen to their comments.

Advertising also shapes consumers' wants, and companies know it. In 2012, companies spent an average of $3.5 million for each thirty-second Super Bowl ad. They spent millions more on other ads.

Notice how most ads feature few details about products. Most technical details wouldn't fit in a thirty-second TV spot. But skillful advertisers can make you laugh in half a minute. They can also appeal to core values: A washing machine frees up family time.

A car takes you on adventures or protects your family. Restaurants provide good times with friends.

Even annoying ads can work. Mucinex's Mr. Mucus may make you groan, but you might think of him the next time you feel sick.

Now vs. Later

College can improve your earnings ability and expand your intellectual horizons. A car might provide flexible and reliable transportation. A new computer can make schoolwork easier.

Big-ticket items like these satisfy real needs. They also cost more money than many consumers have available. Savings and borrowing can help.

When you save for something, you forego spending on that and other items now. Money set aside each week adds up. If it's in a bank account or other form of investment, the money can earn interest. Interest is the amount paid for the temporary use of money. When you deposit money in a bank, the bank can invest it

or make loans to others. The bank pays for this privilege by paying you a percentage of your deposit as interest.

Conversely, when you borrow money, interest pays the lender for letting you use someone else's funds. Borrowing can let you get something now, but you must pay for it later. Bank loans and credit cards are both forms of borrowing. If you can't pay off the balance within any grace period, you'll owe interest. Late payments incur fees, too.

Combining savings and borrowing can be smart for expensive items. Many people use this strategy to buy homes. They save up a down payment of perhaps 20 percent. Then they borrow the rest with a mortgage. If their income can't cover loan payments, however, banks can foreclose on mortgages. For any loan, understand what you will have to pay and when.

Think carefully before using credit cards. Credit cards are convenient, and they eliminate the need to carry cash. Credit cards can also let you get something now, rather than later. Depending on the rates, however, one year's worth of interest and fees could add 20 percent or more to an item's total cost. Failure to pay on time can also hurt your credit rating. Do you want that new speaker system for a higher cost right now? Or, would you rather wait and pay less in the end?

Remember that no purchase decision stands alone. Every decision to use money involves opportunity costs. In other words, if you use a resource for one purpose, you give up the chance to use it for something else. For example, spending $40 on concert tickets means you have $40 less for clothes, snacks, books, or other uses.

Money and time are both valuable resources. Keep your overall priorities in mind as you decide how to spend them.

Every month, consider what you need and want the most. Decide how you will use money for your top-priority items.

Impulse buying is a spontaneous decision to make an unplanned purchase. Even a small amount of impulse buying can upset your financial plans. At its worst, impulse buying can prevent people from purchasing priority items, including basic needs. If shopping becomes a compulsion, seek help from a qualified mental health professional.

Be Smart About Shopping

Do the Math

1. Decide whether each item on the chart is a need or a want for you over the next two months.

2. Rank the items you classify as wants in order of importance to you.

3. Assume that you have $250 to use for each of the next two months. Indicate on the chart how you would use the money for each month. Allot some for savings and charity, too.

Use of Money	Estimated Cost	Want or Need?	Rank Priority?	How much this month?	How much next month?
School Lunch	$54/month				
Bus to school	$45/month				
New pants	$32 per pair				
New shirt(s)	$20 each				
New shoes	$40 per pair				
School supplies	$12 total				
Books/music	$3–8 each				
Movies	$8 each				
Casual restaurant	$10 with tip				
Mobile phone	$30/month				
Amusement Park	$30				
Other?					
Savings					
Charity donations					
			Total	$250.00	$250.00

Compare and Decide

Chapter 3

"20% off!" "Lowest prices of the season."

Ad lines like these have one goal: luring shoppers into buying. Don't assume that a "sale" is always a good deal. If prices were high to start with, even 30 percent off might still cost more than other choices. Compare your options and then decide.

Coupons can save money if you would otherwise buy the advertised item. Just remember to compare the final price with other options.

Even with genuinely lower prices, sales don't always make sense. Do you really need another jacket or more shoes? How often would you wear them? Are the fit and quality good? No sale is a good deal if you won't use and enjoy whatever you buy.

Understand Unit Pricing

Which is a better buy: ten candy bars for $3, or fifteen of the same size and brand for $4? Unit pricing determines the cost for each item of measurement in a package. In this example, one candy bar would be the unit, and the 15-for-$4 package would be the better deal. You'd pay about 27¢ per bar instead of 30¢.

Bigger packages often offer savings, but that's not always true. Use unit pricing for comparison shopping but consider other factors, too. A larger package may be a bad deal if it's unwieldy or has too much waste.

Unit pricing is especially helpful for comparing brand name and generic products. Generic means something belongs to a general class of products, instead of a specific brand. For example, Advil is a specific brand of the generic drug ibuprofen.

Consider Quality

Sometimes you won't need—or easily afford—top-of-the-line products. A paperback novel may be just as enjoyable as the hardcover version. It travels easily, too!

Often prestige pumps up a product's price. A department store purse may be similar to a designer model—except for the designer name and price tag.

Sometimes products' qualities vary widely. For example, some toilet paper brands are stronger. Some are softer. Some break down better in septic systems. Decide which qualities matter most to you and how much you're willing to pay for them.

Review expert ratings for purchases that are expensive or out of the ordinary. The consumer advocacy group Consumers Union tests

many products and publishes results in *Consumer Reports*. Sites like CNET offer specialized reviews of computers and electronic products. Recalls.gov provides information about any product recalls—instances where manufacturers take back products for safety or other reasons.

The reliability of nonexpert users' reviews on the Internet varies widely. Nonetheless, it helps to know about other people's experiences.

Don't assume that Internet search engines list the best sellers first. Search engines often list sponsored links first. Companies pay for those top listings. After that, computerized rules called algorithms determine the order of results. Price and quality often don't factor into those calculations.

Investigate All the Costs

When comparing costs, factor in shipping, maintenance, service, and other fees. For mobile phones, for example, don't just look at a phone's advertised price. Review any required data and service plan, too.

Internet shopping expands consumers' options. However, you can't try on or inspect online products before purchase. Make sure you understand sellers' shipping charges and return policies. Then compare online and other options.

Also, think about nonmonetary costs, including the opportunity cost of your time. Saving $1 across town isn't a good

Be Smart About Shopping

deal if getting there takes an hour in traffic. You could be doing other things in that time!

Explore Other Options

Sometimes borrowing makes more sense than buying. Growing high school guys typically rent tuxedoes for the prom. Some students rent textbooks for college courses.

Deciding whether to buy or lease a home is an important choice. Renting allows more flexibility if people plan to move soon. Renters don't need a huge down payment and have less responsibility for maintenance. Buyers own their home after paying off any mortgage. Many homeowners can deduct mortgage interest on tax returns.

Leasing or buying a car is another big decision. Leasing lets people get a new car every few years, and monthly payments can be lower than those for a purchase loan. However, leases can impose hefty fees for extra mileage, early termination, or excess wear and tear.

In barter, people swap goods or services with each other. For example, someone might provide three weeks' worth of frozen meals in return for a handmade bookcase. Both parties purchase something—but not for cash.

Making something is another alternative to buying. Just remember to consider all the costs. A homemade cake usually costs less money, but the opportunity cost is the time you spend baking.

Make comparison shopping a regular habit. Even small savings will add up, making it easier to satisfy your financial needs. You'll have more flexibility for your financial wish list, too.

Even the cheapest item is a poor choice if it doesn't deliver value for the money. Nor does a high price tag guarantee good quality. Savvy comparison shopping involves weighing the pros and cons of available options. Then make choices that fit your budget and needs.

Be Smart About Shopping

Do the Math

Decide which choice is best for each situation. Explain your reasons.

1. For after-school snacks, you prefer the taste of Grand-ola brand granola bars to Brand X. Your grocery offers:

   a. Individual bars of Grand-ola bars for $.40 each
   b. A 12-pack of Grand-ola bars for $3.75
   c. A 10-pack of Brand X for $3.59

2. You need new jeans. The store has your size in the Blue Jeans and Designer Duds brands, and both fit well. The best available size for the Prestige Pants brand looks too baggy. Prices are:

   a. Blue Jeans at its regular price of $39 per pair
   b. Designer Duds, usually $50 per pair, on sale at 2 pairs for $67
   c. Prestige Pants, usually $65 per pair, on sale for $29 per pair

3. You lost the A/C charger for your cell phone and need a new one. You also want a new earbud/microphone set for hands-free phone conversations.

   a. Buy Buy offers the charger for $30. It also offers a high-quality earbud/microphone set for $40 and a medium-quality set for $27.

   b. E-Vent is an online vendor that offers the same charger for $29. It offers a high-quality earbud/microphone set for $40 and a medium-quality set for $23. Shipping and handling charges are $7 for either set.

   c. Buy-Line is another online vendor. It offers the same charger for $30. Buy-Line does not offer a medium-quality earbud/microphone set. Its high-quality earbud/microphone set is $38. However, if you buy it at the same time as the phone charger, the combined price for both items is just $51. Overnight shipping and handling is free for orders over $50.

Buyer, Beware!

Chapter 4

"Today All iPads 90% Off."

"Get in shape without setting foot in a gym!"

If something sounds too good to be true, it probably is! Unfortunately, people want to believe. They want something for nothing. They want to get rich quick. They want a miracle cure. While con artists make money, consumers lose out.

Other people are just careless. They don't bother reading fine print on financial documents. Or, they give away private information.

Laws forbid the worst offenses, and government agencies do take action. For the year ending in February 2012, the Federal Trade Commission (FTC) got companies and people who broke the law to give up $223.7 million in unlawful gains. Government orders directed them to pay $9.75 million more in civil penalties. Such actions helped 1.5 million consumers.

Nonetheless, the FTC fielded more than half a million consumer complaints that year.

Even vigorous agency action couldn't recoup everyone's losses.

The best way to avoid a bad deal is not to make it in the first place. Make *caveat emptor* your shopping motto. In English it means, "Buyer, beware!"

Stretching the Truth

If an acne remedy claims "87 percent saw results in just 3 days," stop and think. Who were the 87 percent? What results did they see? How did rival products perform?

Puffery is a subjective claim that is difficult to disprove. Advertisers often use puffery. While puffery isn't exactly lying, it's not necessarily the truth.

Be especially skeptical about health claims. After Reebok and Sketchers made unsupported claims about their toning shoes, the companies settled complaints by the FTC and various states for millions of dollars. While both companies denied any wrongdoing, the message for consumers is clear: Don't fall for quirky claims.

Treat any celebrity endorsements skeptically, too. Celebrities often receive fees to promote products.

Also, remember that what you see isn't always what you get. When *Consumer Reports* compared food package photos with the actual products, the results were disappointing. A microwave sandwich that oozed chunky filling on the package was barely half full. Snack cakes were about half the size pictured.

Read the Fine Print

Be sure to read and understand any contract or other financial document before signing it. Also, read any warranties, notices, or other documents for any significant transaction.

This rule includes major purchases, such as computers, cars, or furniture. It also applies to things like opening a bank account, getting a credit card, taking out a loan, arranging for insurance, renting or buying a new home, or contracting for repair work. Usually the documents' terms govern the deal—regardless of what salespeople say.

If you don't understand something, ask questions. For major transactions, such as the purchase of a home or a mortgage, have a lawyer review the documents. He or she might suggest terms to protect you better.

Beware of anyone who discourages you from seeking independent input—whether it's consulting an attorney or getting a mechanic to inspect a used car.

It's better to spend a smaller amount of money up front than to pay much bigger bills later.

Don't rush into financial decisions either. Walk away from anyone who pressures you to sign on the dotted line. Contracts are legally binding agreements. Make sure you can live with their terms.

Resist telephone callers' sales pressure, too. Ask them to remove you from their call list. Join the FTC's National Do Not Call Registry.

Keep your personal information private. The more information you volunteer to strangers, the easier it is for crooks to commit identity theft.

Identity theft is the fraudulent use of someone else's personal information for gain. Criminals impersonate people by using their birth dates, social security numbers, addresses, phone numbers, or other information.

The FTC's Consumer Sentinel Network received more than a quarter million identity theft complaints in 2010. More than 18,000 complaints came from teens. Even if you're not on the hook for stolen amounts, identity theft can wreak havoc with your credit rating when you apply for college loans or your own credit card. Credit ratings are scores that companies use to judge who is a good risk when making loans or extending credit.

Online social media sites like Facebook and Twitter encourage you to share everything, but too much sharing can harm you financially. Change privacy settings from site defaults so that only your friends can see postings. Never disclose your full birth date, address, phone number, or other information that could let criminals guess your passwords.

Be Smart About Shopping

Don't fall for the lie that shoplifting and employee theft only hurt big corporations. Shoplifters steal more than $13 billion worth of goods each year, says the National Association for Shoplifting Prevention. Employee fraud and theft costs companies more than $450 billion per year, reports the Association of Certified Fraud Examiners.

When people pilfer from companies, it hurts us all. In order to stay in business and make a profit, companies must recoup losses from fraud and theft. Thus, businesses build these expenses into the prices charged to honest customers. The thieves may get something for nothing, but everyone else pays the price.

Do the Math

An online ad touted new computers for as little as $29. Clicking on the ad took you to a web site. The site said you, too, could get a great deal. All you had to do was register and start bidding.

Without reading any of the fine print at the bottom of the screen, you registered with your name, e-mail, home address, date of birth, credit card number, and a bank account number "for verification." Next, you clicked to get the right to make 100 ten-cent bids. Then you joined an auction for a new computer.

Each time you made a bid, someone else bid ten cents more. Every bid reset the auction clock for another six hours. Over the next four days, other bidders kept outbidding you. Someone named Betty Buy seemed to bid around the clock. When you had used all your bids, you got another packet of 100 ten-cent bids. After using half those bids, you gave up following the auction.

When your credit card bill arrived, its charges included a gottagetadeal.con membership fee of $89. The site also charged $0.98 for each ten-cent bid in your 100-bid packets, whether you used them all or not.

1. How much did your unsuccessful experience on the penny auction site cost you?

2. Suppose eleven more people registered for the site and bought a packet of 100 bids to take part in the same auction. One of them finally got the computer for $72.30, including shipping and handling. How much did the successful bidder spend?

3. How much did the site's operators charge you and the other eleven bidders over the course of the auction?

4. What warning signs could have alerted you to possible problems with gottagetadeal.con?

Be Smart About Shopping

Know Your Rights

Even the best efforts can't guarantee total satisfaction with your purchases. Know how to stand up for your rights when things go wrong.

Promises, Promises

Warranties are promises by sellers or manufacturers. Breach of an express or implied warranty can make a seller or manufacturer liable for damages that result.

Express warranties are spelled out in written contracts or product documents. Some companies ask you to mail in a postcard or complete an online form with your name, address, purchase date, and similar information. Such registration might not be necessary, but it's usually wise in case a safety recall occurs.

Implied warranties arise by law. All fifty states and the District of Columbia have adopted laws called the Uniform Commercial Code (UCC). Article 2 of the UCC deals with sales of goods.

The UCC holds merchants to an implied warranty of merchantability. Among other things, this means that goods are

fit for their ordinary purposes. The warranty also means goods are packaged and labeled honestly and adequately.

In some cases, the UCC also imposes an implied warranty of fitness for a particular purpose. The seller must know or have reason to know: (a) that the buyer will use a product for a particular purpose; and (b) that the buyer is relying on the seller's skill or judgment.

In certain cases, the UCC lets sellers limit their liability. Sometimes the law also lets sellers exclude all warranties. In those cases, sellers must use clear language, such as "with faults" or "as is." In general, buyers must also have a chance to inspect goods before purchase.

Voice Your Complaints

When something breaks down, don't get mad. Get even—not in an angry way but financially.

Start with a written complaint. Check the sales documents or contact customer service by phone or online to determine how and where to send your complaint.

Write about your problem in clear, concise language. What is the product? When did you get it? What went wrong with it? What happened as a result?

Ask the manufacturer or store to fix the problem. Say if you want to return the product for a refund. Or, ask for a replacement or repair. Request a response within a reasonable time.

If a company's first response isn't helpful, speak to a supervisor or manager. If that doesn't work, contact the business owner or corporate headquarters. Be truthful, polite, and persistent.

Companies usually won't provide refunds, repairs, or replacements if a consumer misused a product or if an express warranty expired. However, there are exceptions. If the manufacturer's negligence caused personal injury, for example, it might still be liable.

If repeated repairs don't solve a problem with a new motor vehicle, that vehicle may be a "lemon"—a seriously defective automobile. Even if the manufacturer's warranty has expired, the federal Moss Magnuson Warranty Act and similar state "lemon laws" may require companies to replace the vehicle or to allow a return and refund. Companies may also owe certain out-of-pocket costs.

Problem products aren't the only area for possible complaints. Contact companies if you get shoddy service, experience payment problems, or have an insurance, banking, or credit card dispute. Make notes about any phone conversations and keep copies of letters or emails.

If diligent efforts don't resolve a problem in a reasonable time, consider contacting a government agency. For example, a state public utilities commission might investigate electrical service problems. Licensing agencies review complaints against various

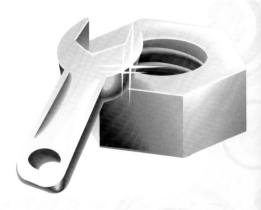

professional and business contractors. Consumer advocacy offices at the state and local levels sometimes act as go-betweens to mediate disputes.

Private business and consumer groups can also help. The Better Business Bureau's online complaint process deals with many kinds of businesses, as well as complaints about charities. Media outlets in the Call for Action Network investigate and report on consumer problems. Professional groups, such as local bar associations or medical associations, may also investigate complaints.

If other avenues fail, file a complaint with the Federal Trade Commission and any relevant state consumer protection agency. Sometimes agencies can get refunds or other relief for consumers. Even if they can't, agency action could protect other consumers by shutting down unscrupulous businesses.

I'll See You in Court!

If other efforts don't solve a problem, consider taking your case to court. If you're still under eighteen, talk a parent or guardian first, though. Going to court is a serious matter, and people who file lawsuits have various responsibilities.

Small claims courts handle many consumer claims up to certain limits. Those limits range from $2,500 to $25,000, depending on the state. Small claims court filing fees are generally lower than for other types of cases. In simple cases, plaintiffs can often represent themselves.

For other lawsuits or complex small claims cases, you may need an attorney. Local bar associations can provide referrals.

Ask about all fees and costs before hiring a lawyer. Request a forthright evaluation of your case and the timeline for possible recovery. Sadly, the time and expected expenses sometimes outweigh the realistic prospects for recovery.

Keep all financial papers organized in a safe place. Have separate folders for receipts, warranties, bank statements, repair records, tax filings, and so on.

If problems or questions arise, send copies of relevant paperwork. Keep the original documents in your files.

Mounting debt and credit problems can dig people deeper and deeper into financial trouble. No matter how bad the situation is, ignoring financial problems will only make them worse.

Even if you contributed to a problem, get help. The Association of Independent Consumer Credit Counseling Agencies helps consumers find nonprofit counseling groups in their areas.

Be Smart About Shopping

Do the Math

To further your budding photography career, you saved up for a year and bought a Hot Shotz brand Single Lens Reflex Digital Camera, plus two special lenses. The camera's sale price was $400. A telephoto lens cost $80, and a wide-angle lens cost $50. The factory warranty period is one year. You paid an extra $40 to Buy Buy to extend the warranty to two years, including all service costs on repairs. Sales tax was 8 percent on everything.

You've had the camera six months now, and it's been in for repairs five times. Three times the problem was a stuck shutter. Twice the built-in flash failed. Buy Buy took ten days to repair the camera each time. Each time it broke down again within three weeks.

Now you want to return the camera for a full refund and buy another brand elsewhere. The telephoto and wide-angle lenses won't fit on the other brand's model, so you also want to return those for a full refund. Buy Buy's store manager has refused to cooperate.

Write complaint letters to corporate headquarters at both Buy Buy and Hot Shotz. Set out the facts and ask for a full refund of all money paid. Each letter should show that a copy is also going to the other company.

Consider the Bigger Picture

We all depend on others every day. Other people in our communities rely on us, too. Civic financial responsibility is how smart consumers answer society's needs.

The Price of Civilized Society

Suppose there were no roads, bridges, or any form of public transportation? What if America had no public schools, libraries, or police departments?

It's hard to imagine America without these and other public programs paid for by taxes. As Supreme Court Justice Oliver Wendell Holmes wrote: "Taxes are what we pay for civilized society."

Progressive taxes impose higher tax rates on those who can better afford to pay. Under the federal income tax, people with more earned income pay a higher marginal tax rate than those who earn less. The marginal tax rate is the rate for each extra dollar of earned income. Income that falls within lower brackets incurs a lower tax rate.

Be Smart About Shopping

To illustrate, suppose the tax rates for a single person were 10 percent for income up to $8,700, 15 percent for additional income up to $35,350, and 25 percent for additional income up to $85,650. Next, suppose someone's taxable income—after taking into account all deductions and credits—is $50,000, and all of it comes from wages. That person would pay $870 in taxes on the first $8,700, $3,997.50 on the next $26,650, and $3,662.50 on the last $14,650.

A flat-rate sales tax is a regressive tax. Although everyone pays the same rate, the tax imposes a relatively bigger burden on lower-income people. For example, if one person earns $150 per week and another earns $450, then $15 in sales tax takes three times as big a bite percentage-wise from the first person's paycheck.

Questions about tax policy are subject to ongoing public debate. Nonetheless, even people who disagree with the tax laws must pay or face the consequences. Billionaire Leona Helmsley reportedly once quipped, "Only the little people pay taxes." When the government proved the hotel owner committed tax evasion, Helmsley went to prison.

Federal law sets April 15 as the deadline for filing individual income tax returns. By law, most businesses withhold part of employees' income during the year and send it to the government for them. If your job doesn't require withholding, either ask for it, or make sure you save enough to pay your taxes by April 15.

Tax rules and forms are often complex. If you seek help, choose a reputable, established accountant, lawyer, or tax preparation service. Con artists sometimes charge unsuspecting taxpayers hefty fees for filing fraudulent returns. When they take off, victims remain on the hook for all taxes, plus potential penalties.

Share the Wealth

Helping others can make a huge difference in your community, country, and the world at large. When preparing to make donations, compare and choose carefully among organizations that seek your help. After all, you want your money to do the most good.

Review annual reports and other information about organizations' programs. Ask how much groups spend on administration and fund-raising. Review information on the organizations' Internet sites. Also, check ratings from groups, such as Charity Navigator and the Better Business Bureau.

Be skeptical if financial information about an organization is not easily accessible. Accountability and transparency help show that a nonprofit group handles funds responsibly. Reluctance to disclose information could signal a possible scam.

Fraudulent organizations' names sometimes sound like those of real charities. Con artists might use fake sweepstakes to lure donors. Or, they may pretend you owe money for a "thank-you gift." You have no obligation to pay for unsolicited merchandise.

Resist high-pressure tactics from any organization. Even if a phone fund-raiser sounds legitimate, avoid impulsive pledges or donations. Instead, review options for charitable giving when you update your budget. Make decisions that fit with your overall financial plans.

Consider Corporate Responsibility

During the late 1960s, more than 14 million consumers boycotted table grapes. Their action pressured California farm owners to bargain collectively with the United Farmworkers Organizing Committee. Consequently, laborers got better working conditions. Consumer activism continues today.

Some companies have stellar track records for supporting responsible environmental practices, fair wages for workers, and other goals. For example, Starbucks Coffee Company requires growers to meet sustainable farming standards—methods that can continue over the long run. "We were willing to pay a premium for coffee that helps protect the environment," said Sue Mecklenberg, former vice president for sustainable procurement at Starbucks Coffee Company.

Other companies have profited directly or indirectly from child labor, forced labor, and hazardous practices. In 2012, the *New York Times* reported awful working conditions at factories in China that made parts for Apple's electronic devices.

Whatever cause you support, consider putting your money where your mouth is. Company Internet sites sometimes post corporate responsibility statements. Follow the news, too. Consumers' purchasing power can make a difference.

Remember that you can spend money, you can save it, or you can give it away. Civic financial responsibility involves sharing some of your money with others. That, in turn, makes society better for everyone.

An old saying holds that if you give a man a fish, he will eat for a day. But, if you teach a man to fish, he can eat for a lifetime.

In 2006, the Nobel Peace Prize went to Muhammad Yunus and Grameen Bank for their work in microfinance. Microfinance groups aim to empower people through entrepreneurship. Entrepreneurship involves developing, owning, and managing a business.

Typically, microfinance organizations lend small amounts so people in developing countries can start a business. When the business succeeds, owners can support themselves and help their area develop more. As people repay loans, the microfinance organization can help more people.

Don't think that only rich people should have a will. Wills, life insurance, and other planning tools make it easier for families to deal with the financial aftermath of death. Plan to make a will once you're eighteen or the minimum age specified by your state's law.

Review and revise the will periodically. Include important nonfinancial provisions, too, such as naming a guardian for any young children.

Be Smart About Shopping

Do the Math

How would you respond in each situation? Explain your answer.

1. Your cousin phones from out of state and asks you to pledge $1 per mile for a 20-mile walkathon. You have a total of $15 budgeted for charitable donations this month. You usually give $1 each week to a collection for the local hunger center.

   a. How much more than your budgeted amount would you owe if you make the pledge and your cousin completes the walk?

   b. How could you respond if your cousin pressures you to make a pledge right now at the $1 per mile level?

2. Suppose you earn $5,000 over the year at part-time and summer jobs. Suppose also that federal, state, and local income and other taxes add up to 10 percent of the total.

   a. What is your income after taxes?

   b. How much would you be donating if you gave 5 percent of your after-tax income to charities?

$ Glossary

barter—Alternative to a cash transaction, wherein people swap goods or services.

boycott—Refusal to buy or use a product, often for social policy reasons.

credit—Arrangement that lets a buyer obtain something now in return for promising to repay a lender later, including any interest or other fees that become due.

currency—The form of money accepted in a particular country or location.

entrepreneurship—Developing, owning, and managing a business.

generic—Belonging to a general class of products, as opposed to a specific or brand-name item.

identity theft—Fraudulent use of someone else's personal information for gain.

grace period—A period of time beyond a due date during which a financial obligation may be met without penalty or cancellation.

interest—The amount paid for the temporary use of money.

"lemon law"—Federal or state consumer protection law that applies to vehicles with persistent problems.

microfinance—Providing loans and other financial services to low-income people to help them rise out of poverty.

mortgage loan—A secured loan, usually to pay for a house or land.

needs—Things people must have to survive and function normally in society.

opportunity cost—What someone foregoes by using a resource, such as money or time, for one purpose instead of others.

progressive taxes—Taxes that place a heavier relative burden on people with better ability to pay.

puffery—Exaggerated sales claim that is hard to disprove.

recoup—Regain.

taxes—Amounts collected by government for public programs.

unit pricing—Calculating the cost for each item of measurement in a package.

wants—In consumer spending, things that people desire beyond basic needs.

warranties—Promises by sellers or manufacturers.

Learn More

Books

Bellenir, Karen, ed. *Cash and Credit Information for Teens: Tips for a Successful Financial Life*. Detroit: Omnigraphics, 2009.

Butler, Tamsen. *The Complete Guide to Personal Finance: For Teenagers*. Ocala, Fla.: Atlantic Publishing Group, 2010.

Lawrence, Lane, and Tom Ridgway. *Buying Goods and Services*. New York: Rosen Central, 2011.

Scheff, Anna. *Shopping Smarts: How to Choose Wisely, Find Bargains, Spot Swindles, and More*. Minneapolis, Minn.: Twenty-First Century Books, 2012.

Internet Addresses

Federal Trade Commission
   <http://www.ftc.gov/>

Junior Achievement Student Center
   <http://studentcenter.ja.org/Pages/default.aspx>

MyMoney.gov
   <http://www.mymoney.gov/>

Do the Math Answer Key

Chapter 1: It's Your Money

Answers will vary. Double-check arithmetic to make sure addition and subtraction are correct. Most students purchase notebooks, pens, books, and other school supplies. Many also purchase new clothes. New computers, phones, calculators, or other electronics might also be on the shopping list. Purchases causing regret might be clothes that were uncomfortable or supplies that were not necessary.

Chapter 2: Decide on Priorities

Answers will vary, depending on individual circumstances. Here's how one teen's worksheet might look:

Use of Money	Estimated Cost	Want or Need?	Rank Priority?	How much this month?	How much next month?
School Lunch	$54/month	Need	1	$54	$54
Bus to school	$45/month	Need	2	$45	$45
New pants	$32 per pair	Need 1/ Want 1	5/10	$32	$32
New shirt(s)	$20 each	Want 2	12		
New shoes	$40/pair	Need 1	4	$40	
School supplies	$12 total	Need 1 set	6	$12	
Books/music	$3–8 each	Want 6	11		$11
Movies	$8 each	Want 2	7	$8	$8
Casual restaurant	$10 with tip	Want 2	9		$10
Mobile phone	$30/month	Need	3	$30	$30
Amusement Park	$30	Want	8		$30
Other?					
Savings				$14	$15
Charity donations				$15	$15
			Total	$250.00	$250.00

Chapter 3: Compare and Decide

1. b: The 12-pack of Grand-ola bars for $3.75 is a better buy if you eat them regularly, because it costs $1.05 less than 12 individual bars. While Brand X costs $0.16 less per dozen, you don't like them as much, so don't buy them.

2. b: Designer Duds on sale at 2 pairs for $67 offers better unit pricing than one pair of Blue Jeans at $39 per pair. While Prestige Pants costs $10 less per pair, they don't fit well, so skip them.

3. c: The combo deal from Buy-Line provides a better quality earbud/microphone set and costs $6 less than the medium quality set and charger from Buy Buy.

Chapter 4: Buyer, Beware!

1. $89 + $98 + $98 = $285

2. $89 + $98 + $72.30 = $259.30

3. $285 + $259.30 + (10 x $187) = $2,414.30

4. The $29 ad price should raise suspicions because it sounds too good to be true. Reading the fine print before submitting any personal and financial information could have alerted you that getting a membership and entering the auction would cost at least $187.

Chapter 5: Know Your Rights

Answers will vary. The letter should be in a business letter format, including name, date, address, name and address of the company, a greeting such as "Dear Sir or Ma'am," and a signature.

The body of the letter should calmly explain the facts. A separate paragraph should request relief. In this case, you want a refund for the camera's sale price, along with the price of the extended warranty, the lenses, and sales tax. The total for these items is $615.60.

Be Smart About Shopping

Chapter 6: Consider the Bigger Picture

1. a. $5

   b. Resist people who pressure you to make a financial commitment right away. One possible response would be to decline altogether because you can't afford to give as your cousin requests. Or, you might say the requested amount is beyond your budget, but you'll review your finances and get back to your cousin later to say whether you can support the cause at a lower pledge rate.

2. a. $4,500. Multiply $5,000 by 0.1, which is 10 percent, to get $500, and then subtract that from $5,000 to get $4,500.

   b. $225. Multiply $4,500 by 0.05, which is 5 percent, to get $225.

Index

A

advertising, 5, 11–12, 16, 23–24

B

bank loans, 12–13
bartering, 19
Better Business Bureau, 32, 38
borrowing, 12–13, 19
buyer beware (caveat emptor), 22–26

C

celebrity endorsements, 23
charity, 38
comparison shopping, 16–20
complaints, 30–32
Consumer Reports, 17–18, 24
corporate responsibility, 39
costs, investigating, 18–19
coupons, 16
court, 32–33
credit cards, 12–13
credit ratings, 26

D

Do The Math, 9, 15, 21, 28, 35, 41

E

entrepreneurship, 40

F

Federal Trade Commission (FTC), 22, 32
financial papers, 34
financial problems, 34
financial review, planning, 8, 40
fine print (contracts), 24–25
fraud, 27

G

goods, 6–7

I

identity theft, 26
impulse buying, 14
interest, 12–13

L

lawyers, 33
leasing, 19
lemon laws, 31

M

microfinance, 40
money, 6–7
mortgages, 18, 19
motivations, 11–12, 22

N

needs vs. wants, 10–11
negotiations, 7

O

opportunity costs, 18, 19

P

price, 7
priorities, 10–14
product reviews, 17–18
puffery, 23–24

Q

quality, value, 17–18, 20

R

renting, 19

S

sales, 16
saving, 12–13
search engines, 18
services, 6–7
shoplifting, 27
small claims court, 33
social media, 26
supply/demand, law of, 7

T

taxes, 36–38
theft, 27

U

Uniform Commercial Code (UCC), 29–30
unit pricing, 16–17

W

warranties, 29–31
wills, 40

Be Smart About Shopping